I Wonder Why

Pets

Hannah Wilson and John Butler

KINGFISHER

NEW YORK

flip the flaps

Copyright © 2009 by Macmillan Children's Books
KINGFISHER
Published in the United States by Kingfisher,
an imprint of Henry Holt and Company LLC,
175 Fifth Avenue, New York, New York 10010.
First published in Great Britain by Kingfisher Publications plc,
an imprint of Macmillan Children's Books, London.

Distributed in Canada by H. B. Fenn and Company Ltd.

Library of Congress Cataloging-in-Publication Data has been applied for.

ISBN: 978-0-7534-6286-7

Kingfisher books are available for special promotions and premiums.
For details contact: Director of Special Markets, Holtzbrinck Publishers.

Printed in China
10 9 8 7 6 5 4 3 2 1
1TR/0908/MPA/UNTD/157MA/C

Consultant: Nicola Davies

Contents

Caring for pets

Pets can be a lot of fun, but they can also be hard work. Cats, dogs, guinea pigs, hamsters, rabbits, birds, ponies, and horses all need love and care, just like you do.

cat

cat carrier

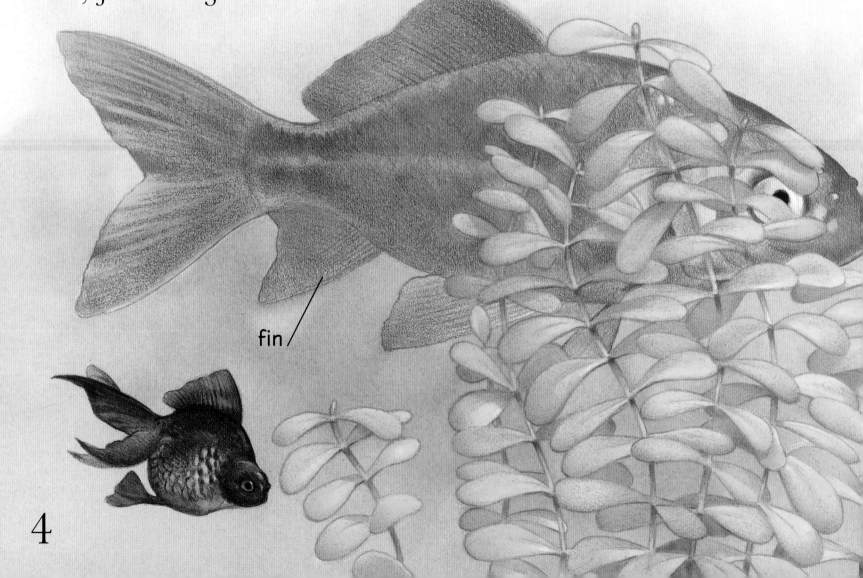

fin

4

1. When do you need to use a cat carrier?

2. How do I take care of my pet?

3. Which pet has fins?

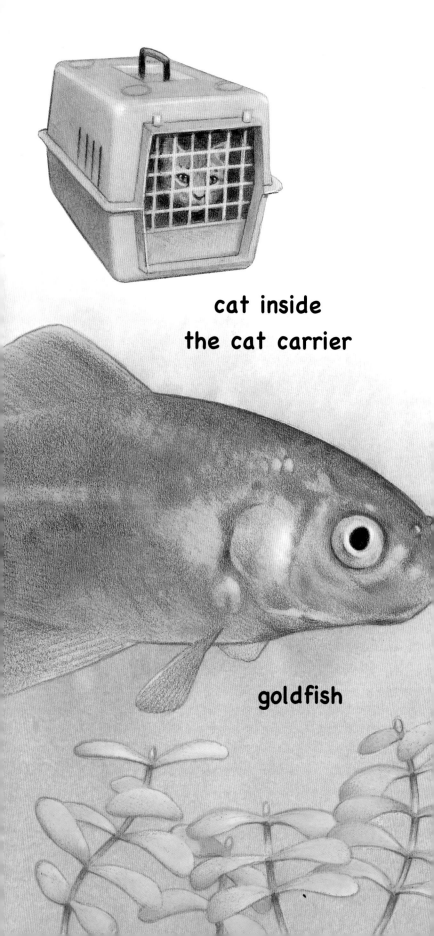

cat inside
the cat carrier

goldfish

1. When pets are sick, they need to go to the vet. A cat can be carried to the vet in a cat carrier.

2. All pets need the right food to eat, fresh water to drink, and somewhere warm, safe, and clean to sleep.

3. A goldfish has shiny golden fins. They help it swim.

A dog needs . . .

a bone to chew

fresh water to drink

a clean basket to sleep in

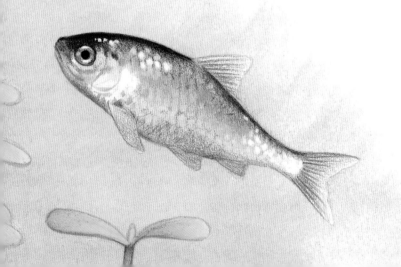

5

Cats

Cats like to explore and
play, but they also like
to find a warm spot where
they can curl up and sleep.
Most cats love being stroked,
especially behind their ears
and under their chins!

soft toy
on a string

cat getting
ready to jump

cat sleeping

6

1. Why do cats like toys that move?

2. How high can a cat jump?

3. How does a cat clean itself?

jumping to
reach the toy

1. Cats like to chase moving toys because it is like hunting real mice!

2. A cat can jump up onto a fence as tall as a person!

3. A cat can clean itself by licking. It also stretches and scratches things to keep its claws sharp.

A cat likes to . . .

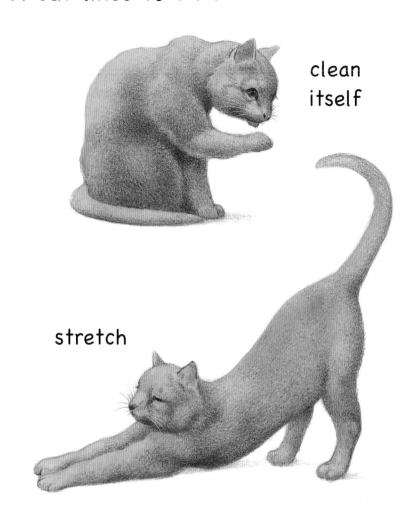

clean itself

stretch

scratch a post to keep its claws sharp

7

Dogs

Puppies, or baby dogs, love to play. They enjoy chasing a ball or running around inside or outside. All dogs need a lot of exercise and can be fun friends to take out for a walk.

muddy
Old English
sheepdog

dalmatian
puppies

waiting to
go for
a walk

8

1. When does a dog need a bath?

2. How many types of dogs are there?

3. How do puppies play?

all clean and
brushed

1. A dog needs a bath around once each month—or whenever it gets muddy.

2. There are around 400 types, or breeds, of dogs. They can be big or small, shaggy or smooth haired. Some even have curly tails!

3. Puppies like to roll around together and chase a ball.

puppies playing with a ball

Some breeds of dogs

pug

Norfolk terrier

poodle

cocker spaniel

dachshund

9

Hamsters and guinea pigs

Small, silky hamsters and soft, furry guinea pigs are shy animals. They need big cages with a lot of hiding places where they can sleep.

hungry golden, or Syrian, hamster

seeds

hamster running on a wheel

10

1. Where does a hamster store its food?

2. How do hamsters stay healthy?

3. What does a guinea pig eat for dinner?

hamster crawling into a tunnel

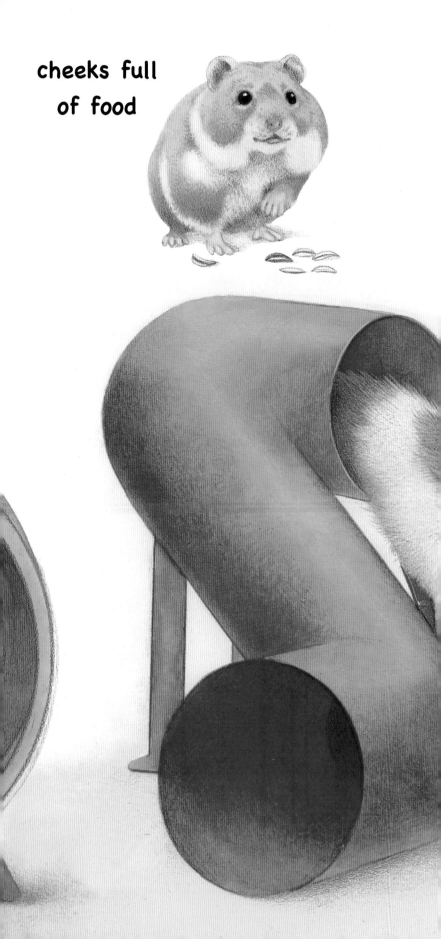

cheeks full
of food

1. A hamster stores its food in its cheeks. It eats nuts, seeds, and fruit.

2. Hamsters stay healthy by running on exercise wheels and scampering through tunnels.

3. A guinea pig eats hay, fresh grass, vegetables, and pellets. It also drinks plenty of water.

crawling out of the tunnel

A guinea pig likes to . . .

eat hay

munch pellets

drink fresh water

11

Rabbits

Fluffy, twitchy-nosed rabbits have strong back legs to help them hop and big teeth to gnaw and nibble their food.

hutch

fence ————

hopping along the grass

eating dandelion leaves

1. Where do rabbits live?

2. What do rabbits eat?

3. Why do rabbits have
long ears?

leaving the
hutch

nibbling
a carrot

1. Rabbits live in a hutch. During the day, they can hop around in a safe, fenced area of the yard.

2. Rabbits eat grass. They also munch hay, pellets, carrots, apples, and dandelion leaves.

3. All rabbits have big, long ears to help them hear better.

Rabbit ears can be . . .

pretty long

long

very long and floppy

13

Birds

Pet birds need a cage with lots of room to stretch out their wings and fly around. Friendly parakeets, or budgies, can be trained to fly around a room and even land on your finger!

male parakeet

female parakeet

perch

14

1. Why do parakeets snuggle up together?

2. What is the difference between a male and a female parakeet?

3. What keeps a zebra finch happy?

parakeets snuggling
up together

1. Parakeets like to live with a friend. They clean each other's feathers with their beaks.

2. A male parakeet has a blue patch on the top of his beak. A female's patch is pinkish-brown.

3. A zebra finch likes to eat millet seeds, splash around in a bath, and fly around.

A zebra finch is happy . . .

pecking at millet seeds

splashing in a bath

flying

15

Ponies and horses

A pony is a small horse, but it's still very big! Ponies and horses need a lot of space to live in and plenty of grass and hay to eat. Ponies and horses need their coat, mane, and tail brushed and hooves cleaned.

mane

tail

hooves

pony in a field

16

1. Where do ponies and horses live?

2. What do ponies and horses wear when they go for a ride?

3. When is a pony or horse a chestnut?

riding a pony

saddle

1. Ponies and horses live in fields or stables.

2. A pony or horse wears a seat called a saddle. The rider controls the pony or horse with reins attached to a bridle.

bridle

reins

3. A chestnut pony or horse is reddish-brown. Other pony and horse colors also have special names.

fitting a saddle to a pony

Different colors of ponies and horses

chestnut (reddish-brown)

bay (dark brown)

piebald (black and white)

17

Index